CENTER FOR
THE STUDY OF
FOREIGN AFFAIRS

BLACK LABOR UNIONS IN SOUTH AFRICA
REPORT OF A SYMPOSIUM

Edited by
Anthony G. Freeman and
Diane B. Bendahmane

1987

FOREIGN SERVICE INSTITUTE
U.S. DEPARTMENT OF STATE

The views expressed in this publication are solely those of the authors and do not necessarily represent the views of the Center for the Study of Foreign Affairs or the Department of State.

Library of Congress Number: 86-600599

Department of State Publication
Foreign Service Institute
Center for the Study of Foreign Affairs

Released October 1986.

Contents

Preface

In the past two years South Africa has been thrusting itself toward the center of the stage of world affairs. Imprisonments, bannings, strikes, demonstrations, ever stricter controls on the press, and the mounting death toll among both blacks and whites—these are the surface manifestations of the unrest and change taking place in South Africa.

Black labor unions have been playing an important role in these changes, especially since the sweeping changes brought about in 1979 by the government's enactment of the Wiehahn Commission's recommendations, which made black labor unions legal. As this book is going to press, union employees of the Ford Motor Company in Port Elizabeth have walked off the job demanding a say in the management after Ford carries out its divestment plans. At the same time, 25,000-35,000 striking black miners from three gold mines rejected as inadequate pay increases of up to 23 percent. Their union, the National Union of Mineworkers, represents 500,000 black miners at 18 gold mines and 11 coal mines.

This book, which examines the current status of black labor unions in South Africa and their potential for effecting change in that troubled country, is based on a symposium co-sponsored by the Center for the Study of Foreign Affairs and the State Department's Bureau of Intelligence and Research on April 30, 1985. The contributors—all participants in the symposium—are competent academics; many have spent their lives studying South African affairs. Their perspectives are invaluable for people involved in U.S. policy toward South Africa. As one of the contributors points out, South Africa is the only nation in Africa in which a well-developed, mature labor movement has played or is playing a role in a national liberation movement. Understanding the roots and current status of this vibrant movement is essential.

The symposium on black labor in South Africa was one among many that the Center for the Study of Foreign Affairs has organized since its inception as a new division of the Foreign Service Institute in 1982. These symposia have focussed on U.S.-Soviet relations; science, technology, and foreign affairs; international negotiation; transition from dictatorship; economics; and a number of U.S. bilateral relationships. In addition to the symposia, the Center offers a facility for foreign affairs personnel to carry out research and also conducts a foreign policy simulation program for the Department of State. Many of the Center's activities lead to publication.

Thanks are due to Drs. Marshall Trip of the Bureau of Intelligence and Research and John Collier of the Foreign Service Institute who organized this symposium and to Anthony Freeman who provided the excellent introduction.

Stephen Low
Director
Foreign Service Institute
October, 1986

1.

Introduction

Anthony G. Freeman

Black labor unions in South Africa is a topic of considerable interest to policymakers on South Africa who recognize that the industrial work force has often served as a catalyst for political progress and social change in the developing world. It was not uncommon for leaders of the postwar political independence movements to have come out of the ranks of organized labor. Thomas Mboya of Kenya, Sekou Toure of Guinea and Joshua Nkomo of Zimbabwe are a few of the many prominent nationalist leaders who rose from labor positions. The trade unions were training grounds and early vehicles of political expression as they were often the only form of organized activity permitted by the colonial authorities. The colonial powers tolerated them because they were necessary for the orderly conduct of industrial relations. Native unions were granted concessions that would have been inconceivable at the time for nationalist political movements. Organized labor in the metropolitan countries supported the native unions and pressured their respective governments to make such concessions. Thus the emerging unions in the colonial territories typically assumed dual roles as partners in industrial relations and political action groups.

The independent black trade union movement which emerged in South Africa as a result of the Wiehahn Commission recommendations of 1979 represents in the words of the AFL-CIO's Lane Kirkland, "the best hope for the peaceful dismantling of apartheid," i.e., by industrial and political action instead of burning "necklaces" and all-out civil war.

Since they were officially recognized in 1979, black unions have made unprecedented gains, which they continue to consolidate. For example, a progressive Industrial Court has shown itself capable of producing judgements of major importance such as the Marievale gold mine decision of 1985 which strengthened the protections afforded legal strikers. Also, the government is committed to abolishing the last vestiges of legally sanctioned skilled job reservation for whites in the mining industry before the end of 1986.

While the pace has been uncertain and evokes skepticism, this industrial progress has been accompanied by significant political reforms such as the end of the pass laws and influx control. But the regime has no timetable nor clear idea of what system of political power-sharing

Mr. Freeman is Special Assistant to the Secretary and Coordinator of International Labor Affairs at the Department of State.

2 Anthony G. Freeman

it intends to put in place—except perhaps that it should be along federal or ethnic lines and not based on one-man/one vote in a unitary state, presumably in order to divide the blacks and preserve the hegemony of "the white tribe." Moreover, the regime's instinct is to react perversely to rising black discontent and foreign pressure. South Africa continues to paint a surrealistic checkerboard landscape, with its Third World black homelands and townships and First World industrial/financial base and modern white suburbia.

The industrial relations reforms of 1979 produced a revolution of rising expectations among black workers who continue to encounter the restrictions of the apartheid system once they leave the factory gate. In the absence of any real participation in the central government of South Africa, blacks look to the new unions as quasi-political articulators of their interests and grievances.

The unions have become increasingly politicized during the past few years, especially since the two states of emergency which were ushered in, beginning with the violent wave of reaction to the elections for the three parliaments, white, colored, and Asian, that swept through the black townships in the fall of 1984. While intended by Pretoria as a provisional step on the road to greater political reform, it was the blatant exclusion of blacks from the South African tricameral constitutions which, together with the economic recession, helped ignite black rioting in late 1984.

The new trade unions were swept up as well and somewhat reluctantly agreed to participate in the work stayaway of November 5-6, 1984, in the Transvaal area. Momentarily chastened by strong government and employer reaction to that protest, the black unions failed to support a United Democratic Front-sponsored work stayaway in Port Elizabeth in March 1985. But since then they have come increasingly under pressure from the worker rank and file and undoubtedly from the UDF as well to respond to the government's countermeasures against the worsening township unrest and adopt a more activist stance. Work stayaways and consumer boycotts became the order of the day and massive detentions of black union and political militants followed. Pretoria's uncompromising attitude on black political rights blurred the line further between labor and politics, and the partial success in trade union unity efforts brought about the emergence of a "superfederation" in November 1985.

While the black labor movement is still in its infant stage and badly fractured, the union's power is growing, all factions oppose apartheid, and there is increasing willingness to act directly against the government. Black unions do not yet have the strength to force the government to accelerate political reforms, but the threat of a prolonged general strike is no longer a fantasy.

In the face of this crisis, a curious business-labor coalition is developing. Both sides need strong and effective collective bargaining, but white management's concern is not just over those aspects of apartheid that constrain economic growth. With the spectre of black power looming somewhere over the horizon, progressive business elements also sought to accelerate the reform and negotiation track—or at least hedge their bets for the future—by opening a dialogue with the African National Congress (ANC)-in-exile in September 1985.

It should be emphasized, however, that full-scale black revolution is not immediately around the corner. The white state is a regional economic and military giant. Its armed forces have the might to prevail on all its borders with the "front line" states—whose economies are linked closely with and dependent on South Africa's economy—and at the same time keep the homelands and seething black townships bottled up. South Africa's State of Emergency detention laws enable it to roll up and decapitate the black labor leadership quickly when deemed necessary.

After the upsurge in trade union militancy, the other key political achievement of the black labor movement has been the move towards trade union unity. Called COSATU (Congress of South African Trade Unions), the "superfederation" launched in November 1985 represents a merger of the National Union of Mineworkers (NUM), the largest single union in the country; the shop floor-oriented, industrial-based unions that formerly made up the FOSATU (Federation of South African Trade Unions) labor federation; and the politically activist "general worker" type unions linked to the UDF political umbrella. Claiming some 450,000 members at the outset, COSATU is now the largest black union federation in the country. The philosophy said to bind COSATU together is "nonracialism," but a perhaps more important characteristic which the UDF unions bring to this venture is their anti-capitalist ideology and neo-Marxist rhetoric.

Left out of this coalition were the officially "nonracial" but "black consciousness-leaning" Council of Unions of South Africa (CUSA) and the strongly "black consciousness" Azanian Confederation of Trade Unions (AZACTU) linked to the AZAPO political movement. The latter two labor federations have now formally merged together forming a rival pole called CUSA-AZACTU with a claimed membership of over 400,000 workers.

COSATU adopted a highly visible political profile from the outset, lending credence to the perception that it had been hijacked by the UDF, in turn considered by many as a political front for the underground ANC. Among COSATU's avowed aims is to force divestment of foreign capital as a means of bringing the apartheid state to its knees.

Since May 1986 there has been a third pole added to the black union equation, known as UWUSA (United Workers Union of South

Africa). UWUSA is a product of the violence-prone political rivalry between the UDF and the Inkatha movement of Zulu chief Gatsha Buthelezi who, reacting to COSATU's pro-UDF tilt, has decided to counter it by building his own labor arm. UWUSA today numbers perhaps no more than 50,000 workers, but it is supported by the militant Inkatha which is over a million strong. While anti-apartheid, UWUSA espouses a pro-free enterprise, anti-disinvestment philosophy.

Another recent development has been the breakup of the oldest trade union federation in South Africa, the pre-Wiehahn, middle-of-the-road, "multiracial" TUCSA (Trade Union Council of South Africa). Claiming a 500,000 membership in 1983, TUCSA's black and colored unions have defected because of continued white, particularly Afrikaaner, domination of its leadership. It remains to be seen whether the white workers will join forces with the right-wing, all-white South African Confederation of Labor.

There is a tendency to paint COSATU as organized labor's wave of the future. Indeed, CUSA leaders do not rule out the possibility of an eventual merger with COSATU. Since CUSA's merger with AZACTU, its rhetoric sounds more like that of COSATU's and it has taken a harder line in favor of economic sanctions and against foreign investment. But there is an uneasy relationship within COSATU between the "workerist" FOSATU unions and the smaller but politically militant UDF faction, which could become exacerbated if the latter pushes the struggle for black political power to the point where the state threatens to retaliate by annulling the black unions' hard-earned industrial bargaining rights. Moreover, it is estimated that the existing unions have organized only about a quarter of the total "organizable" labor force. The organizational structure of the black trade union movement is by no means settled yet; there will be more organizing of the unorganized, more splits, and more mergers.

While the black labor movement may be deeply rooted in African traditions, its international relations are becoming increasingly important. South African apartheid has become a prominent issue in European and U.S. domestic politics. There is a complex interrelationship between black political and labor groups inside South Africa and important political and labor center in Europe and the United States, albeit some of these are in the opposition, as in the United States. As the black labor movement has become more articulate—and more nihilistic, I would add—in demanding foreign sanctions and disinvestment, it has pressed the democratic international labor movement to put pressure in turn on Western governments, including the United States, to impose economic penalties on the apartheid regime. Under the influence of the black labor movement, the AFL-CIO and the labor international to which it belongs, the International Confederation of Free Trade Unions (ICFTU), have

U.S. Public Strongly Opposed to Apartheid

South Africa has just become a part of the prayer at Howard University chapel. The same is true of other churches here in Washington, D.C.—Shiloh, Plymouth— I'm speaking of the black community, but it's no different in the white community. South Africa is, if not part of the catechism or a part of the prayer, part of the reality that feeling, thinking, religious people are trying to address.

The issue is being discussed in school and university classrooms, seminaries, corporate board rooms, and city councils across the country.

Simply said, a lot of people in the United States, right or wrong, think that apartheid and what flows from it is morally objectionable—just plain wrong—and that the United States should have as little to do with South Africa as possible.

Ronald Palmer

moved, along with other currents of Western political opinion, from halting support of partial disinvestment to a full fledged call for a coordinated international boycott. One result has been the recent comprehensive and anti-apartheid legislation in the U.S. Congress.

There is also a growing international aid relationship. From the Western camp the ICFTU provides assistance to its affiliate in South Africa, CUSA. With financial support from the U.S. government, the AFL-CIO gives additional aid to CUSA and other independent shop floor-oriented black unions, including some that are affiliated with COSATU. But the COSATU top leadership rejects assistance from the ICFTU proper, let alone the Americans, preferring to take its aid directly from the ICFTU's European affiliates, particularly the Scandinavian unions who use funds donated by their respective governments.

It should be noted that with the growing polarization it is becoming more difficult for Westerners to maintain contact with both the South African government and the black opposition. UDF leader Rev. Allan Boesak, for example, refused to meet with Coretta Scott King unless

Ambassador Palmer is a Visiting Scholar and Senior Fellow at the Georgetown University Center for Strategic and International Studies. He moderated the morning session of the symposium.

she renounced her intention to see State President P.W. Botha and Chief Buthelezi. COSATU eschews AFL-CIO aid because of the Reagan Administration's "constructive engagement" policy. For its part, the South African regime casts an increasingly hostile eye on foreign assistance for the black unions.

On the communist side of the ledger there is an historic alliance involving overlapping positions between the ANC leadership, now exiled in Lusaka, and the South African Communist Party. The Soviets provide covert military aid and training; and the ANC's official labor arm, SACTU (South African Congress of Trade Unions), is formally affiliated to the Soviet international labor front, the WFTU (World Federation of Trade Unions). But the Western-oriented ICFTU recognizes that the ANC constitutes the prevailing political culture in South Africa's urban black townships today and has initiated a dialogue with the ANC leadership (sans SACTU) in Lusaka.

This raises still unanswered questions as to the prevailing political philosophy underlying a black trade union movement which vaguely calls itself "Africanist" and "socialist." It has borrowed ideas from West European social democratic experience such as "worker control" in the factories, but what political model will it espouse—Western pluralistic democracy or the systems we see elsewhere in Africa and other Third World countries that are more akin to the Soviet model: one leader, one party, one union, all marching in step?

Will tribalism play an important role or has the advanced stage of South Africa's industrialization process already effectively submerged ethnic differences among urban labor? How will the labor movement handle the inherent conflict between labor and political goals? Will it balance these interests in order to continue taking advantage of the benefits of the state-sanctioned industrial relations system, or will it inevitably surrender itself to all-out revolutionary aims? And what of its tentative relationship with white capital—will it seek pragmatic alliances, or will it revert to ideological form and treat white capital as the handmaiden of apartheid? Now that international sanctions are being imposed, will the labor movement accept responsibility for and be willing to sustain the loss in jobs eventually implied by foreign disinvestment, or will this produce a backlash in the labor movement? Will labor retain its autonomy of the black political forces and even lead the struggle for power-sharing, or will it eventually be subordinated to a mass political movement?

These are some of the questions that are considered in the following chapters.

2.

From the ICU to the
Wiehahn Commission

Barbara Harmel

The history of black trade unions in South Africa between their first emergence in the Industrial and Commercial Workers Union (ICU) and the appointment by the South African government of the Wiehahn Commission is, at one level, a record of the long and difficult struggle of the black South Africans to win legal recognition of their representative bodies. But because these black workers are also black inhabitants of a country which has, for centuries, discriminated against them on the grounds of their color, their struggle has gone far beyond the traditional, so-called "bread and butter" issues.

Black trade union history in South Africa is also one of alliances with the broader political movements for national liberation. While the nature of those alliances has undergone several changes over the decades, the racist character of South African society has always made it inevitable that black trade unions confront broader political issues. Black workers have been embroiled in a dual fight: the traditional battle for wage increases and improved working conditions, together with that for the removal of a discriminatory legislative system based on race.

During the 60 years between the creation of the first black trade union in South Africa and the establishment of the Wiehahn Commission—for investigating and making recommendations on the conditions of black trade unions—black workers have made impressive gains. Most significant among them are first, their degree of organization, which ultimately won them legal recognition, and second, clarification of their relationship, as trade unionists, to the broad political movement. It is to this development of political power, in regard both to the white polity and the black national liberation movement, that this chapter addresses itself.

Dr. Harmel is Director of the U.S. Africa Commission at the Center for Development Policy.

7

Beginnings

The first national trade union organization of black workers in South Africa was the Industrial and Commercial Workers Union of Africa (ICU), established in 1919. Created by Clements Kadalie, a native of then Nyasaland (now Malawi), the ICU was born in the wake of World War I, during which local industry had been considerably stimulated, increasing the size of the black working class.

Initially the ICU restricted itself solely to trade union issues, partly to avoid conflict with the national liberation movement, the Native National Congress (now the African National Congress) that was formed in 1912—the oldest national liberation movement on the African continent. However, at that time, the ANC was very much an elitist organization, dominated by professionals and chiefs who were anxious to differentiate themselves from the masses. The ICU began to fill the political gap created by the ANC's failure to mobilize the masses politically. As a broad umbrella organization, it peaked by 1927 with a membership of 100,000.

A number of reasons have been given for the decline of the ICU, the most common being Kadalie's leadership—at once heavy-handed and financially mismanaged. No doubt the Depression also contributed to the collapse of the ICU. But, perhaps most significant among the causes for a rapid fall in ICU membership, was the 1924 Industrial Conciliation Act. Passed by the coalition government—Labour and National Parties—then in power, the act stipulated that legal recognition could could be given to whites-only trade unions. This meant that only white unions were legally entitled to participate in the process of collective bargaining. All black unions were excluded from this process.

Growth and Restructuring

While the black urban working class was not very large during the 1920s, it had already manifested a considerable appreciation of the principles of trade unionism, as well as a populist political sentiment somewhat akin to that of the American Industrial Workers of the World. The 1930s ushered in a period of regrouping along industrial lines for black trade unions. As the Depression lifted, the labor force began to swell, rising by 58 percent in the manufacturing sector from 192,420 in 1932 to 303,557 by 1936. While blacks remained outside the scope of industrial conciliation procedures, they began to discover ways to obtain some form of protection. Resorting increasingly to strikes, the number of which rose from 12 in 1934 to 34 in 1937, blacks found responses to their applications for wage determinations more and more favorable.

The pressure from black trade unions for legal recognition nevertheless continued to intensify. A small gain was made under the 1937

Wage Act through which "interested persons" were granted an opportunity to make representation before a labor board. The board, however, did not welcome individual workers, because it believed they had little knowledge of methods of wage fixation and as a rule were not able to gather information, whether statistical or otherwise, on a sufficiently extensive scale to be of use to the board. As a result, the board encouraged bodies of workers to appear before it, and regarded this as de facto recognition of black trade unions.

During the 1930s black political movements entered a period of quiescence. No black political movement was addressing itself to the issue of black trade unions. At that time the only umbrella movement was the South African Trade and Labor Council, which itself was having enormous difficulties in coordinating trade unions in South Africa. As I mentioned, the 1924 Industrial Conciliation Act had driven a wedge into trade unionism in South Africa along racial lines. Whites were beginning to perceive that it was in their interest to separate themselves from black workers.

The Impact of World War II

By the end of the decade of the thirties, when World War II broke out, enormous changes took place which were to have a tremendous impact both on the African National Congress and on National Party policy. South African local industry was greatly stimulated by the outbreak of World War II, and, as a result, the number of black workers in South African manufacturing increased by 53 percent, and black trade unions swelled. Jan Smuts, then prime minister, demonstrated an interest in the allied war effort and adopted and encouraged a policy of allowing blacks to go into urban areas to obtain jobs in manufacturing. It is probably true that Smuts may have had no choice in the matter since he did not have an administration which could have effectively administered the influx controls on the statutes at the time. Nevertheless, he was also not anxious to have the influx controls enforced because the manufacturing industry needed at their disposal as large a labor force as they possibly could muster.

Black trade unions flourished during World War II as a result of Smuts's policy. Strikes were very quickly brought to an end, for management was no more in favor of extended disruptions than was the state at the time. In these circumstances, black wages rose more rapidly than ever before. The gap between white and black wages narrowed for the first time, and, by the end of the war, the single largest coordinating party, the Council of Non-European Trade Unions, claimed a membership of almost 160,000.

The African National Congress was watching this process, particularly its younger generation which was led by people who have now

become familiar to anyone who knows something about South Africa—
Nelson Mandela, Oliver Tambo, and Walter Sisulu. The National Party
was also watching. Both groups were focused on the growth of a massive,
organized black labor force; one group was highly excited about the potential of black labor, the other was highly intimidated by it.

The African National Congress Youth League started agitating
for the parent body to turn its attention to mass mobilization and to lay
aside the petitions and delegations that had occupied it since its inception in 1912. For its part the National Party began to focus on the dangers
of what one of its theorists described as the growth of a "native pro-
letariat" in South Africa.

National Party policies became very focused during World War
II. The party was supported by a number of sectors that were interested
in restricting the size of and the political implications of a black working class in South Africa. White farmers were desperate because of the
loss of workers who during the war years had poured into the urban
areas where wages were much higher than they were on the farms. White
workers were threatened socially by a large black presence in the towns,
and also in terms of competition on the shop floor. In fact, the National
Party came into power in 1948 by wooing both white farmers and white
workers on a platform of restricting the black labor force as well as a
black political labor force in the towns.

Once in power, the National Party attempted to set up Labor
Bureaus in South Africa, the function of which were to restrict the
numbers of blacks who could legitimately come into the urban areas.
However, the system did not get off the ground. For obvious reasons
Africans did not want voluntarily to register with the Labor Bureau,
nor did the United Party-appointed administration want to cooperate in
the process. Therefore, the National Party was not able to get the system
going overnight and the Labor Bureaus themselves did not become functional during the 1950s.

Instead the National Party turned to the pass system as a way of
achieving the same goal: preventing labor from coming into the towns.
And in 1950 the National Party passed the Suppression of Communism
Act, which was used primarily against leaders of the trade union movement. These efforts to weaken organized black labor in South Africa
were highly successful.

The Growth of Black Political Activity

In the 1950s the African National Congress turned its attention
seriously towards organizing and mobilizing a mass black political move-

ment in South Africa. The main undertakings of the ANC during the 1950s are fairly well known: the Defiance Campaign of 1952, which first sparked off the ANC into a mass movement (it claimed a membership of about 100,000 at the end of the campaign); the Congress of the People in 1955, at which the Freedom Charter was adopted; and the attack on the Bantu education system. Through the 1950s the ANC challenged many aspects of the Party policy of apartheid, but the ANC did not focus on labor.

The only coordinating body of black trade unions during the 1950s was the South African Congress of Trade Unions (SACTU), which saw its role as part of the umbrella organization of the Congress Alliance. (Member organizations of the alliance were the ANC, the Coloured People's Congress, the Indian Congress, the Congress of Democrats (white), and SACTU.) It did not take any independent political action during the 1950s but regarded itself primarily as the bread-and-butter trade union wing of the ANC. In turn, the ANC paid very little attention to the trade union movement during the 1950s. In fact, during the 1950s, the trade union movement in South Africa often felt itself overshadowed, neglected, and at times even exploited by the ANC, which called on workers to join mass demonstrations or strikes or stay-at-homes but otherwise ignored them. The trade unions felt that there was not an equal partnership between the ANC and SACTU in decisionmaking. This antagonism reached a head in 1958 when the ANC called on SACTU to help organize a three-day stay-at-home and at the end of the first day declared it unsuccessful and called it off without consulting SACTU.

While the ANC and SACTU never actually split, for a long time the trade union movement in South Africa saw itself as "used" by a strictly political movement that was interested, not in labor, but only in mass political pressure on the South African government.

Labor Recognizes the Power of Its Own Position

In 1960 the ANC finally turned, as did the Pan-African Congress, to the crucial issue of the pass system. The South African regime cracked down hard on the opposition forces. A state of emergency was declared after the shooting of 69 people at Sharpeville by the police. The ANC and the Pan-African Congress were banned permanently, and during the 1960s a reign of terror was instituted in South Africa. Prisoners were tortured and held in solitary confinement without trial as a fairly standard practice. For a very long time thereafter the South African economy boomed, and there was little evidence of an opposition movement from either labor or political forces.

This hiatus in opposition activities came to an end in 1972, when the labor movement re-emerged in South Africa. Until the formation of the United Democratic Front, there was no strong political coordinating movement in South Africa, and labor came to recognize the power of its position, particularly as Africans filled more and more skilled jobs. Today labor movement members feel that they will determine their own political action and will not be dictated to by any outside political group. They are certainly prepared to cooperate at some levels with it, but they are not going to fall back into the position they had in the 1950s.

The re-emergence of militancy in South Africa during the 1970s was in part a reflection of the changing position of black workers in the labor structure. The need for skilled labor had grown increasingly desperate, and, in the absence of sufficient numbers of white immigrants, blacks were drawn into performing skilled jobs. While this shift was not accompanied by a concomitant increase in wages for blacks doing skilled labor, it was a significant structural change. Skilled black labor represented employer investment and could not easily be replaced. Hence, a larger and larger proportion of black workers were moving into a far more powerful position in the labor market.

In the face of this growing militancy, the government took a decision, based on the recommendations of the Wiehahn Commission, finally to grant legal recognition to black unions. The intent behind the decision was to create "tame" black trade unions that would be co-opted by the conciliatory machinery extended to them. The government was certainly not unaware of the double-edged potential of granting legal recognition to black unions—that against the possibilities of co-option lay the threat of a tightly organized and powerful black labor movement. Many restrictions accompanied the new recognition as a result.

There is a debate within the African National Congress as to how to cope with the current situation. One faction wants to intensify the armed struggle and even start to focus on "soft-targets," as they call them. (Even after adopting armed struggle in 1961, the ANC's policy was to restrict its targets to "hard targets"—pylons, railway lines, military installations—and to avoid taking human life. As the level of state violence increased during 1985-86, the ANC began to consider attacking military and police agents.) Another faction wants to maintain the level of armed struggle that currently exists; and a third wants to abandon armed struggle and devote its resources entirely to strengthening the labor movement in South Africa.

The National Party government's response to the beast in its midst on which it depends, appears to be two-fold. On the one hand there has been the by now classic response to opposition—a major crack-down on labor leaders, many of whom have been in detention since the imposition of the state of emergency. But on the other hand, the government seems still to believe that it has sufficient time on its hands to buy off black unionized labor. The specter of mass unemployment and deportations from the urban areas in a weakened economy are some of the sticks to be used in the battle to gain quiescence from the black labor movement. These same sticks, however, have provided fuel to the growing momentum of resistance among black South Africans—a momentum the black trade unions are unlikely to be excluded from.

Conclusion

It has become increasingly clear, in the six years since black unions won recognition, that many difficulties have continued to dog their movement. Far more important, however, the black trade union movement has mushroomed and flourished. Against considerable odds it has built an unprecedented unity among different unions and has maintained a markedly democratic dynamic between leadership and rank and file members. Forty years after the black labor movement made its first critical impact on both the ANC and the National Party, both of these organizations are again faced with a major challenge emanating from this now far larger and more powerful movement.

3.

The Wiehahn Commission

Stanley B. Greenberg

It is not an overstatement to say that the black labor movement in South Africa is the most vibrant labor movement in the world today. In terms of growth, it is hard to imagine any other industrializing or industrialized nation that has witnessed such a rapid growth of trade union movements in such a short time.

This vibrancy, however, is evident in more than numbers. There is a vitality to the organizational process in South Africa that reminds one of early nineteenth century Britain and late nineteenth century-early twentieth century United States. In the segregated townships there is a rich, deep cultural vibrancy based on a mixture of traditional culture and labor movement or working class culture. Turning back this movement through political suppression will be very difficult because its roots are very deep in the community. The organizational forums that bargain in the workplace are just one aspect of a very rich, integrated labor movement.

The Commission's Recommendations

After the general strikes of 1973 and 1974 and the 1976-77 Soweto disorders and their aftermath, the Wiehahn Commission of Inquiry was appointed by the government in 1977 to report on labor legislation. Its report was published in 1979.

The report called for incorporating African workers into the industrial relations structure that had been in place for whites, coloreds, and Asians since 1924. The industrial conciliation machinery had proved successful in incorporating white workers who, in the period 1920 to 1924, were experimenting with various political forums including socialist forums. After that institutional machinery was established in 1924, the unrest, the growing political consciousness of white workers was quelled and they were incorporated into the establishment without any difficulty.

Dr. Greenberg is Associate Director of the Southern African Research Program at Yale University.

The Wiehahn Commission of Inquiry

The Wiehahn Commission was appointed in 1977 to investigate labor. Its recommendations, issued in 1979 and by and large accepted by the South African government, instituted sweeping changes in African industrial relations.

Changes brought about by the Wiehahn recommendations are as follows:

1. *All Africans are eligible to join and form registered unions. (Initially migrant laborers were excluded.)*
2. *The racial composition of a union and its executive body is decided by the union alone. (Initially the government required racially separate branches and an all-white executive body for multiracial unions.)*
3. *Agreements entered into by unregistered unions have no legal validity, and employers may not deduct dues for such unions.*
4. *New mechanisms are created and old ones revised:*
   * *present industrial councils can veto new unions or employer bodies wishing to join*
   * *one union, one vote replaces proportional representation on industrial councils*
   * *liaison committees are to be called "works councils"*
   * *the National Manpower Commission and the Industrial Court were created to review labor relations issues that arise from the changes in the system and to interpret labor law and adjudicate in cases of labor disputes*
5. *Restrictions on the political activities of registered unions are broadened.*
6. *Jobs may no longer be reserved by statute for whites. (Existing job reservation determinations are to be phased out.)*
7. *Africans working anywhere in South Africa are eligible to become artisan apprentices.*

The Wiehahn Commission apparently intended to try to follow that example by extending that institutional machinery to African workers. The Commission hoped that, by becoming part of a bureaucratic system of self-management in industry, African workers would limit their demands and utilize the established system rather than political agencies to seek redress of grievances.

The Wiehahn Commission's solution was based on a fairly narrow view of history in that it assumed that what had worked for white workers would work just as well for black. White workers, unlike their black counterparts, however, had political rights and their conciliation machinery was established in a period of ample resources and a political economy which allowed the government to protect white workers and subsidize industries that employed them—the whole process of uplifting poor whites. But the context was quite different in 1979 when the system was set up for African workers. Blacks did not have political rights, nor were the resources available to uplift this large a proportion of the population (approximately three-quarters of the working class).

A Honeymoon for the South African Labor Movement

One has to be cautious in predicting whether or not the government plan for incorporating African labor will in fact bring about a tame South African working class, which thinks only of bread-and-butter issues. The regime is severely limited in its ability to respond to what is actually happening in South Africa. Currently the government and the African labor movement are on a honeymoon. It is a time when pent-up demands for organization are being met as the state and business have provided a fair amount of freedom for trade unions to organize. There is certainly not complete freedom; nevertheless, it is striking, given the nature of this regime, how much freedom there is to organize within a clear legal framework. In addition, because the trade union movement was effectively smashed in the 1950s and 1960s, now there is a tremendous concentration on plant-level organization, rather than on political demands.

But this honeymoon is not likely to last long. First, it is not reasonable to assume that the state will continue to allow the labor movement so much freedom. There is clearly a great deal of controversy within South Africa over how much freedom to provide. One day the prime minister talks about freeing Mandela, the next he jails the leaders of the United Democratic Front. I suspect there is a similar struggle over how to respond to African trade union organizations. Current estimates of membership range from 600,000 to 800,000.

The Objectives of the Wiehahn Reforms

Question: *What were the white government's objectives in instituting the Wiehahn Commission reforms in 1979? To what extent have those objectives been achieved?*

Wilmot James: *The government incorporated African workers into the industrial conciliation machinery because it was faced with an ungovernable industrial situation. It was an attempt to create institutions by which African labor could more predictably become part of a new set of industrial relations.*

The outcome is mixed. On the one hand, there has been a regularization of industrial relations, but at the same time African workers have cultivated a space for themselves of the sort that is not exactly functional in terms of government control. Government's response to that has been that these are teething problems which any industrializing country will go through.

Pearl-Alice Marsh: *Recently we have seen more use of legal channels by the trade unions; however, we need to reserve judgement as to whether or not government's attempt to bring the trade unions into the legal industrial conciliation system can be called a success. Labor has been forced to use official channels because of the defensive position they've been placed in in the economic downturn. But if there were an economic upturn, we might again see labor challenging the system more aggressively. We need to extend our observations for a period of time before we make judgements about how effective the Wiehahn reforms have been.*

As pressures on the white regime increase, attempts will be made to tighten the screws on the African labor movement. That will produce predictable responses within the African labor movement itself.

Also management is likely to set limits on the growth of the African labor movements. As mentioned, management, particularly in larger multinational corporations and some larger corporations in South Africa, has given a fair amount of freedom for unions to organize, but it is not clear how long that will go on. Management is not always the principal advocate of labor organization and mobilization. In fact, it is more predictably a restraining force that will try to limit the emergence of a militant African trade union movement.

During the honeymoon, the labor movement's leaders have been able to deliver. For example, the 1985 firing of mine workers was reversed. The unions have been able to obtain wage increases and have won concessions on job security issues. However, as the screws tighten either on the part of the state or on the part of management, trade union leaders may not be so successful in fighting labor's battles.

Ultimately, I believe, the African trade union movement will become politicized, and the Bantustan elites and bureaucracies will have a role in this process. To some extent industry has become concentrated in border areas, homeland areas, where management faces trade unions with fewer rights, where the wage machinery is less developed, and where the opportunity for political suppression is greater and easier to hide. Bantustan leaders may eventually try to intervene as management suppresses trade unions and limits their expansion. This, in turn, may lead industry to relocate into areas where the labor environment is a tougher one for African trade unions to operate. Indeed there is some evidence that the process of relocation has already begun, as an increasing number of manufacturers have taken up the new incentive packages for relocation "deconcentration" points.

Government Intentions and Results

Looking back to 1979 at what the Wiehahn Commission recommended and what the government articulated at the time, it is fairly evident that the government did not get what it intended to get. The government accepted the Commission's recommendation to amend the 1924 Industrial Conciliation Act to permit Africans to join registered unions but rejected the notion that migrant workers would be part of the trade union movement. The industrial conciliation system was reserved for settled urban Africans, a privileged element, a minority of African workers. Naturally, such a system would create basic divisions within the African working class, and African workers themselves swept aside this proposed provision, which the government clearly had no capacity to enforce. Also management was not much interested in defining out migrant workers either, since both settled and migrant workers were employed in the same plants. Management was not interested in coping with two legal systems. Government intention clearly was not able to be enacted and enforced on this point.

It was also clearly the government's intention that parallel unions—African unions organized by the pre-Wiehahn established white and mixed unions— would become the dominant labor forum for African workers. The dominant forum was not to be independent African unions, outside the existing white-controlled federations.

The government clearly aligned itself with the Trade Union Council of South Africa (TUCSA), the largest labor federation, in the hope that it would be able to maintain control over parallel unions. However, as it turned out, parallel unions are almost of no consequence. The government's ability to control the development of the African labor movement has been greatly limited.

The fact that the government did not completely get its way highlights two aspects of the South African labor situation. One is the weakness of the South African state. There's a lot of bravado in the South African state's claims that it is in control. However, as recent events show, the state has not been able to dictate what kind of trade union movement it would have. In fact, the trade union movement operates outside of state control and is in the hands of the African workers who created it. It is a movement that has not only institutional forms, but very deep roots in the community.

The second aspect is the central role played by domestic forces in the emergence of an African trade union movement. There would have been no legal change and no African trade union movement if it were not for the strikes of 1973 and 1974 and the Soweto disorders of 1976. It is tempting to look for a non-conflictual path to change in South Africa, but in reality protest and violence help drive the process of change and are a critical part of it. Business could not see its way clear to align itself with labor reform until it was forced to do so by the mobilization of African workers, and it will not continue to press for reform and to create freedom for reform unless domestic disorder continues. External forces, including protest and divestment campaigns in the United States, support the process of domestic change in South Africa.

There is a process of liberation going on in South Africa. It is not going to end in the next five or ten or even twenty years. The process is very different from what took place in other African states. Central to the process in South Africa is the emergence of an organized African working class. Whatever the strategies of external-based movements, there is a very vibrant African trade union movement which is developing organizations and leadership which eventually will become politicized and militant and which will participate in any future political dispensation. In trying to understand this process in South Africa, one cannot turn readily to other African examples for guidance: nowhere else in Africa has a liberation movement flowered in so industrialized a country where the organized African working class has proved so important to the political process.

4.

A Redistribution of Power in Industrial Relations

Pearl-Alice Marsh

The first and perhaps the most important reform to take place in South Africa under Prime Minister P.W. Botha's government was the 1979 labor legislation which legalized black trade unions. While the importance of the government action is not to be underestimated, the legislation was in reality the tangible evidence of a redistribution of power in industrial relations. This redistribution had been brought about through a turbulent period of confrontation between government, business, and African labor, as government means proved insufficient to address the emerging demands on the system.

Through very difficult processes, an unrecognized pragmatic partnership between black labor and white business emerged which challenged existing laws and eventually caused them to change. In fact, this relationship, rather than the reform policy of the Botha government, has formed the incipient core of social change in South Africa. The partnership itself was riddled with conflict, distrust, and at times betrayal, but the imperatives of production and employment did not allow either labor or management to withdraw completely. In the rather eloquent words of a striking Dunlop worker, "It's like a game where the winner takes all. You throw the stone, he blocks it; you throw another one; he blocks it, but at the same time he's on the offensive. You block again. The difference is that there is no time for the struggle to end. Each minute going by, you both lose something. You lose a finger and by the second week you're a cripple. The same with him. He loses money and profits. So one of you will have to stop and say 'okay.'" White business and black labor struggled through the 1970s and brought about a major restructuring of power relations in the industrial relations system.

Industrial relations systems in a free market economy can be likened to the international relations system. Order is maintained through the balance of power struck among the various interests in the system.

Dr. Marsh is a Ford Foundation Fellow in International Affairs at the Institute for International Studies at the University of California at Berkeley.

Repression of Mass Demonstrations

Question: *How would the South African government react to an effective and massive demonstration on the part of labor?*

Wilmot James: *I don't think the South African government's repressive apparatus outside of the army has the capacity to repress large-scale worker demonstrations. I think they can attempt to do so, but I don't think they will be effective.*

Barbara Harmel: *I'm feeling slightly confused as to why you feel that repressing labor demonstrations is not a possibility while shooting down people in a funeral procession is.*

C. R. D. Halisi: *Repression of African worker organizations at this time has consequences that are quite different from those when student revolts are repressed or even when community-based revolts are repressed. The consequences stretch across sectors of the economy.*
Worker organizations are far more entrenched and have a command over resources that is invaluable and adds to the equation when it comes to calculations about repression. When I speak about repressive forces, I do not mean the army. I think that would change the equation

While a totalitarian government operating a planned economy may maintain industrial control through hierarchical means, a government interacting with a free market economy cannot—at least not for any length of time. This does not imply that the balance in a free market economy is always maintained through a proportional distribution of power. Given predisposing factors within the system, a disproportional distribution will adequately maintain power until those factors change.

An Economic Agenda Based on Apartheid

In South Africa from 1948 until 1979, the government established and maintained a high degree of control over industrial relations, particularly as they pertained to blacks. However, several things occurred to challenge the government's role. Black employment in manufacturing industries grew to over 50 percent of manpower, and at the same *considerably. I mean the security police and the civilian police. They might try to put down a well-organized labor demonstration, but that would be ill-advised and it wouldn't be successful.*

Robert S. Gelbard: *I would like to add briefly to what Drs. James and Halisi have said. Since 1960, there has been an historical reluctance on the part of the South African government to step in on trade union movements in the same way that they have stepped in on community organizations. The organizational bannings have stopped short of the South African Congress of Trade Unions; during the 1973 and 1974 strikes in Durban, the military and the police were very cautious, nothing like what happened in 1976 in Soweto. I'm not sure about the reasons for this greater caution.*

The government seems unable, short of the use of the army, to gain control over, not funeral processions, but stoppages of all kinds by the labor movement. The township disorders are very telling. The South African government has lost control of the townships. One of the principal vehicles for attempting to exercise control were a variety of collaborative groups in the townships which have been effectively circumscribed, and the South African government has not been able to step in effectively to support its allies in the black communities.

---

time manufacturing grew to surpass the combined agricultural and mining sectors of the economy. During this critical period of industrial growth, adjustments in the entire industrial relations system were inevitable. However, rather than allow the system to adjust independently, the government chose to impose its political agenda on the industrial community.

The consequences of this action are quite historic. To make the political system of apartheid viable economically, the government passed the Physical Planning Act of 1967. This act set forth an economic and industrial agenda based on the principles of apartheid. In keeping with the goal of race separation, the act aimed at virtually eliminating

---

Mr. Gelbard is Director of the Office of Southern African Affairs at the State Department.

urban African workers from the white industrial sector. This was to be achieved through a radical industrial decentralization scheme which would move industries to the border and homeland areas, thereby both transferring existing black jobs and creating new ones in those areas.

Section II of the act instituted control over the zoning of existing industrial lands so that their use around existing industrial areas would be curbed. This restricted the creation of urban employment for blacks. According to the minister of labor, by 1969 the government had been able to curtail the creation of some 220,000 jobs for the Africans in metropolitan areas.

Section III restricted the use of African labor in existing and new industries in the so-called controlled areas. To induce industries to move to the border areas, new industries in the metropolitan areas were disallowed if they were to depend too heavily on African labor. Existing industries were to reduce their black-to-white manpower ratios; the appropriate ratio was determined to be 2.5 blacks to one white. While these measures made sense in terms of the overall political objectives, they did not make sense in terms of economic realities.

From 1970 to 1980 the government put $740 billion in direct investments, subsidies, rebates, and other incentives for industries to move to the decentralization areas. It is estimated that the private sector spent a comparable amount. Approximately 35,000 jobs were created in that time, dismally short of the projected number that government predicted. Furthermore, the opportunity cost of this expenditure was such that for every job decentralized, the same capital spent in the metropolitan areas would have created two to five jobs.

Business engaged in heated arguments against the decentralization policies. The *Financial Mail,* a leading business journal, argued that the policy of industrial decentralization in South Africa evolved not so much out of economic necessity, but as the keystone in the implementation of a political policy of separate development. It argued that the effects of the policies were wreaking havoc on industry through "the haphazard rationing of African labor." Industrialist Harry Oppenheimer, Chairman of the Anglo-American Corporation, argued that South Africa could not hold its place in a highly competitive world if it continued to refuse to allow the proper utilization of 80 percent of its labor force.

At the same time, studies found that the average wage bill across industries was climbing. The *Financial Mail* again reported that labor at factor cost reached an unprecedented peak of 67 percent by 1970. This upward swing of recent years has largely been the result of excessive monetary demand by white labor in relation to an artificially tightened labor supply.

A 1970 survey by the steel and engineering industries found that they were short 27,000 workers and in need of some 7,200 skilled workers. The metal industry estimated that between 1970 and 1975 it would need to employ possibly another 100,000 workers. Master builders frequently complained that whites were not only in short supply, but those available were not sufficiently qualified for jobs reserved for them. For example, of the 1,100 apprentices contracted in Durban in 1971, 98 percent of the colored and Asians met the minimum standards, but only 50 percent of the whites did. In order for many whites to be employed, therefore, qualification exemptions had to be granted.

The government was not immune from labor shortages either. By mid-1974 the minister of posts and telegraphs reported that 532 Africans had to serve temporarily as postmen and postal aides in white positions, while another 284 white positions had been permanently converted to black. Vacancies in railways and harbors were running at 19 percent in the bread-and-butter grades and 42 percent in the training and entry grades.

Hampered by the shortage of labor and the high wage demands of white labor, employers turned overseas for recruitment but found that market unsatisfactory in the long run. The alternative was to turn to the black work force.

By the end of the decade, industry had forced the government to eliminate job reservation in all but a few categories. This had been accomplished by both illegally substituting African workers for white workers, and by occasionally overwhelming parts of the industrial system with exemption requests. Thus, rather than abating through the decentralization policies, the dependence on African labor continued to grow. And since the government could not eliminate this dependence, the challenge became how to control it.

Labor Strikes of the 1970s

On the part of African workers, factors which catalyzed action on their part in the 1970s were low wages in the face of rising costs, unsatisfactory working conditions, and inadequate avenues for expressing their grievances. Resentment and frustration over wages and working conditions were the major grievances which precipitated most strikes during the 1970 to 1980 period. In that decade the government reported 1,800 known work stoppages which involved a total of a quarter of a million black workers. According to the minister of labor, the immediate cause of 92 percent of the strikes was low wages. But rather than acknowledge the inadequacy of its wage determination and industrial conciliation system, the government insisted that the strikes were political in nature and demanded that African workers register their grievances through existing governmental channels.

The primary instruments at that time were the liaison committees and the works committees. In addition, the Wage Commission and Industrial Council were a place where Africans could seek representation, but this representation came through the labor officers. However, business rarely used even these means to accord some accommodation to African labor.

Following the 1973 Durban labor strikes, management throughout the country first of all defined the problem that they had encountered as a human relations matter and began to investigate ways to establish committees in order to open up communication channels with African workers. The government reported that in 1973 773 liaison committees, 125 works committees, and three coordinating work councils had been established. The government lauded the effort to create the committee system. The minister of labor argued that because of the committee system, trade unions were unnecessary for black workers in South Africa. He further argued that the committees actually offered more direct contact between management and black workers than trade unions would. After this surge of committee structure formation throughout industry, and after the strike period abated, many firms chose either not to form committees or to neglect those which had been formed. The initial wave of strikes was treated more as an anomaly than as a sign that things were changing in South Africa, and industry returned to the status quo.

Even in companies that made a conscientious effort to make the committees work, their presence did not reduce the likelihood of strikes. During the years that followed, strikes were no more uncommon in establishments with works and liaison committees than they were in those where such committees did not exist. Black workers generally perceived these committees as instruments of management. The absence of a collective bargaining apparatus for African labor left industrial relations quite unpredictable.

Relying on government agencies as the controlling intermediary between management and labor, employers had lost touch with black workers and were unaware of the depth of their grievances and their own vulnerability to the African strike. The labor unrest of the 1970s proved that the existing industrial relations system was inadequate. In spite of a legal prohibition against African trade unions, business was forced to seek and accept them as an alternative solution to its problems.

Though businessmen in South Africa did not display any sign of liberalizing their attitudes toward the African population, their attitudes toward the African workers and their willingness to recognize representative worker organizations changed quite dramatically over the ten-year period from 1970 to 1980. Whether or not to recognize African trade unions consumed a large part of the debate among industrialists during the first half of the decade. In the early part of the 1970s industry generally refused to speak with any African trade union spokespersons and continued to think that government had a solution. On the other hand, a few, like Oppenheimer, argued that recognizing African trade unions was a part of the solution to a larger economic problem that, unless it was dealt with immediately, would destroy the South African economy.

During the 1973 strikes, black trade unions began to emerge and to play a central role in forging negotiations with management. Black unions formed first in the Durban area and immediately spread to the heartland of industry, the Transvaal.

By 1974, leading industrialists, recognizing the changing environment, began calling for a recognition of African trade unions. At that time, the Anglo-American corporate leadership said it was prepared to recognize and negotiate with black trade unions in all its enterprises. However, fears, conflicts, suspicion, accusations, and threats did not abate on the part of managers just because forward thinking business leaders recognized the need to negotiate with black workers. African trade unions represented a threat to managerial power, and the specter of the politicization of the trade union movement haunted managerial discussions. Management represented an even greater threat to black unions, given the historical alliance of government and industry against black interests, but government's unwillingness to legitimize collective bargaining represented the biggest threat. Industry and black labor could not wait for government to change its mind regarding black trade unions. Blacks would have to form them and management would have to recognize them.

Partnership between Management and Black Labor

Thus a new pragmatic partnership came into being through years of volatile confrontation and seemingly untenable bargaining situations. The emergence of the partnership clearly centered around one main issue: establishing conditions for peace and stability in the workplace. Government had clearly failed to provide stability. Codes of conduct had only served as part of a solution. What remained was a need to institutionalize formal procedures to govern the conduct of business and labor during periods of dispute. Black labor and industry met this need by directly negotiating collective bargaining agreements, and eventually industry lost its will to comply with laws that made trade unions illegal. Business struck bargains with illegal unions and honored agreements they negotiated. By 1982 some industries were even discussing the possibility of negotiating industry-wide agreements with black labor.

The Growth of Collective Bargaining

During the early part of the 1970s the South African economy was in a growth cycle. While everyone else profited, African workers found their wage increases to be too little and too late. The wage adjustment boards, in which they had little to no real input, were unresponsive and insensitive. Disappointed workers took the offensive and began to strike. Consequently, industry was forced to concede on the wage question. But negotiating for wages was only a part of the struggle.

Labor leaders also had to gain recognition from management of their institutional legitimacy. They eventually gained this recognition because of management's fear of continued wildcat strikes and loss of confidence in the government's ability to control them. Accustomed to reprisals against their leaders, workers would often walk off the job and refuse to identify leaders or clearly to state their grievances. For management, calling on the police and firing all workers was only a short-range means of restoring order. Two-hour work stoppages, four-hour work stoppages, and one-day work stoppages were all too frequent and too disruptive.

Management needed leaders with whom they could speak and who could speak to the workers and help the rank and file construct negotiable demands and organize collective bargaining strategies.

The first and most important step in this process involved what has been called "attitudinal restructuring." While anger and mutual threats were an inevitable part of the process, success in resolving a conflict was highly dependent on the degree to which both sides could control their antagonisms, develop some level of mutual trust, and finally seek to ensure the integrity of the agreements reached.

An interesting example of this concerned negotiations between the General Workers' Union (stevedores) and the three stevedoring firms. The workers threatened to strike after a long period of unsuccessful discussions with the stevedoring firms. Quickly recognizing an impossible impasse and a rise in antagonism, the Anglo-American Corporation's industrial relations manager for Freight Services, a subsidiary, requested to be dispatched immediately to Capetown. There he intervened, calmed the dispute, and quickly established rapport with the General Workers' Union. Both parties described what developed as a trust relationship. They negotiated an agreement and ended the strike in one day.

Freight Services also made it a lot easier on itself by calculating rather quickly that it could more easily afford a more costly wage package than a lengthy strike. The wage deal negotiated collectively by the firm cost the Anglo-American Corporation substantially less than the other firms, which in the final analysis couldn't afford what they had bargained for.

The trust relationship had to be translated into action for both management and the unions. Management was obliged to seek accommodations from the head office and, more important, to signal "hands off" to the government. The latter was difficult. The goverment security branch became a real menace to both management and the unions and an extraordinary impediment to industrial peace. In many instances, before a negotiated agreement between labor and management could be formally signed, the security branch would have arrested the leaders and sent the work force into a tailspin. Another work stoppage would ensue. Labor had to transfer its trust of management to the rank and file, educating them on the binding nature of the formal agreements and convincing them on occasion that they might have to go against fellow unions to honor their agreements with management.

During the period of the meat workers' strike, the General Workers' Union had just negotiated a successful agreement with the stevedoring firms. When the meat workers asked the GWU to go out on strike, the GWU refused because it felt it had to honor the agreement that it had made with Freight Services. Therefore GWU workers were obliged to go ahead and on-load the meat that was being shipped out of South Africa in defiance of the strike.

At the end of the decade, by the time the government had legalized trade unions, a new collective bargaining system for black workers was in place, negotiated from their position of organized numerical strength and within the vacuum created by ineffective government channels. Black labor, through its own bargaining processes, had increased its share in the industrial balance of power.

A Test of Union Strength

I have suggested that the conflict between the economic situation and the political demands of apartheid in South Africa set the stage for a hard-fought redistribution of power in industrial relations. However, not all industries and unions were affected, nor did they all behave in identical ways. Yet the overwhelming result was that management, not the government, took the initiative in organizing and recognizing black trade unions.

The trade union movement was forged during a strong economic period. Labor took the offensive and by and large won. Now, however, during a major recession the strength of labor unions will be tested. Will they be able to maintain the integrity of their movement in the face of declining membership, much of which has been laid off? Now that management has seized the offensive and put the emphasis on productivity and austerity measures, can the unions develop defensive strategies which will keep them viable?

5.

South African Business: Adjusting to a New Reality

Robert Copp

I would like to develop four general propositions that both South African businesses and South African entities of multinational enterprises would accept.

Proposition One: Collective Bargaining

In South Africa, medium to large enterprises accept collective bargaining and the disputes resolution role of representative trade unions with respect to designated groups of their employees.

We practitioners in the industrial relations area probably bring to the South African situation, highly politicized as it is, certain preconceptions based on our experiences with trade unions in other national settings. Similarly South African enterprises, not having had experience with the collective bargaining process in a free sense, may bring perhaps a different set of preconceptions. Nevertheless a mature or maturing collective bargaining system is primarily concerned with wages and working conditions and the resolution of disputes about them. It is typically a multi-stage grievance procedure that may end with the final remedy either in third-party arbitration or perhaps in a strike. In that sense collective bargaining and the role of the trade union in dealing with workplace problems over which management has some discretion and control is accepted now by most large companies and many medium-sized and small ones.

One of the problems that management has faced in the highly dynamic and diffuse black trade union movement in South Africa is ascertaining majority representativity. A trade union must have some way of demonstrating that it represents a majority of the defined unit of the work force. Unless there is some system of check-off or dues remittance through payroll deductions, it is difficult to demonstrate representativity. The South African system has not matured to the point of having elections

Mr. Copp is International Labor Affairs Associate on the Employee Relations Staff at the World Headquarters of the Ford Motor Company.

The Influx Control Issue

Question: *In the dialogue between the business communi-ty in South Africa and the state, obviously the issue of influx control comes up. What are both sides saying about this issue?*

Robert Copp: *Two years ago the business community took a position on the Orderly Movement of Persons bill. At that time both South African employer or business organizations and notably the American Chamber of Commerce in South Africa took a strong position that the bill should be withdrawn and never enacted. The five-company statement read, "These organizations believe that without a stable, secure, and prosperous work force, the companies' economic potential and political stability cannot be en-sured in the future. In the national interest, these organizations are committed to an ongoing program of legislative reform to give effect to the following goals, one of which is an end to the forced removal of people."*

Comment from the Floor: *The South African govern-ment had become lax on allowing black people to move into urban areas by allowing migrant workers to qualify in terms of Section 10 of the Urban Areas Consolidation Act. After a while when they realized that there were many more migrant workers who qualified to live in ur-ban areas, they tied the influx qualification to housing. This makes it impossible for most migrant laborers to qualify, even within the next ten years. There is a waiting list of 25,000.*

Comment from the Floor: *A special committee of the South African government is looking at the influx laws in particular. Early indications are that what they are toying with is getting rid of the racial component in the influx laws and requiring someone in an urban area or in a rural area that wants to come to an urban area to have a house and a job waiting for them. This would be two steps forward and one step back.*

to determine representativity. But that is a crucial problem for management in the recognition of trade unions.

Generally speaking, most managements are not yet willing to accept trade union representation of their staff or white collar employees. The trade union movement has been most active and most involved with factory or production employees. When management is getting ready to bargain a collective agreement, it is fairly essential not only that it has a representative trade union body with whom to bargain, but also that it has a good understanding of to whom in a designated group of employees the agreed provisions are to apply.

Proposition Two: External Political Issues

While recognizing that many black unions are active politically, management seeks to avoid an intrusion of external political issues into the collective bargaining relationship. This proposition has a couple of weasel phrases in it. What are "external political issues"? I have to confess that we in management are probably defining them pretty much on an ad hoc basis.

Proposition Three: Stability and Predictability

Management, once having agreed to these dispute resolution procedures, seeks adherence to them. Having granted recognition to a trade union, management expects a reasonable degree of stability and predictability. If agreed procedures are to be amended or changed, it should be done in an orderly fashion.

It was the wildcat strike issue that impelled the business community to support the Wiehahn Commission recommendations and to urge the government to enact them. The business community was after a degree of stability in black trade union relationships. Management hoped this stability would evolve through institutionalizing and legalizing black trade unions so that a dispute procedure could evolve and be followed.

Proposition Four: Consolidation

The business community welcomes efforts at voluntary consolidation and rationalization of the black trade union movement. We are not interested in having some kind of a system imposed by the Department of Manpower. We might accept recommendations about this from the Manpower Commission, but I am not even sure that is its role. It is incumbent upon the emerging black trade unions themselves voluntarily to find the bases for their rationalization and consolidation.

The Politicization of Black Labor

Question: *How do you see the future of labor organizations in South Africa in view of existing legislation which restricts the freedom to organize?*

C. R. D. Halisi: *SACTU has always said that the trade union movement will not be able to organize in South Africa. There are limitations and ultimately the government will clamp down on the trade union movement. When that happens the link between the working class and the underground will be strongly confirmed. Business may then find it more convenient to align with the mechanisms of the state for repression and for limiting the trade union movement, but the black labor movement is not going to go away. The kind of political power that it will have and the forms of resistance it will take up will depend upon developments in the country that I certainly cannot predict. However, I would not be surprised if the South African government alienates this movement in some fundamental ways.*

Some people believe that one of the objectives of management is to seek fractionization of the trade union movement, hoping that this will make it a weaker adversary in the collective bargaining process. However, progressive, enlightened firms are in pursuit of stability and therefore welcome the voluntary efforts by the black trade union movement to consolidate and rationalize the structure.

A Dilemma for Multinationals

The changes that Dr. Marsh outlined began occurring in the 1970s. Coincidentally, there was a movement afoot at that time to criticize the behavior of multinational enterprises in host countries. Multinational enterprises are sensitive to such criticisms. What evolved from the debate in the 1970s was that a multinational enterprise behaved best when it followed the norms of the host country.

Those of us who had been working on the government, political, or labor side of the multinational issue had been conditioned by a decade of trying to bring our own behavior in accord with the norms of the host country. Then we came to South Africa where in the labor area

Black Labor Forced Multinationals to Change

In South Africa both domestic and international firms were quite comfortable operating within the norms of South African society. They had a job to do as profit-making concerns and they were there to do it. It was not some sort of moral imperative that jolted them out of that behavior; it was the incentives taken by black trade union and labor organizations that said, "This is not how we're going to do business any longer in South Africa."

Pearl-Alice Marsh

the norms were simply not acceptable. Nonetheless, most of us behaved in accordance with those norms. But by the mid-1970's, probably as a result of the Durban strikes of 1973 and 1974, we began to rethink whether those norms—the Industrial Conciliation Act, in effect—were acceptable. As early as the International Labor Organization's adoption of its tripartite declaration in November 1977, or perhaps even earlier with the adoption of the European Economic Community (EEC) Code of Conduct and the Sullivan Principles in the United States, multinational enterprises accepted that departing from national norms was appropriate to render apartheid less oppressive and to promote equal opportunity in the workplace.

6

The Political Role of the Trade Union Movement

C. R. D. Halisi

Since the early 1980s there has been an interesting and lively debate about the political role of the trade union movement. Of particular contention is its relationship with the community. For example, Sisa Njikelana of the South African Worker's Union questions whether trade unions represent the working class any better than community organizations. Njikelana's comment was in response to an assertion by David Lewis of the General Workers' Union that trade unions were very different in character from political organizations and therefore should not formally affiliate themselves with federations of community organizations such as the United Democratic Front or the National Forum Committee. Lewis argued that community organizations were mostly comprised of activists—individuals or groups of individuals who came together with specific political goals and programs. Trade union leaders, on the other hand, are elected representatives of worker organizations and are dedicated to bringing workers into a disciplined, yet democratic, trade union movement.

In his famous 1982 speech Joe Foster, general secretary of the Federation of South African Trade Unions (FOSATU), laid out a distinctive brand of politics for the trade union movement. Foster argued that the misleading political category called "the community" disguised the often middle class and partisan character of popular politics. Communities are composed of different groups and classes. Therefore, Foster contends, community organizations, more often than not, are the preserve of the urban middle class. Despite the rhetoric many trade unionists believe that unprincipled involvement in community politics will ultimately compromise working-class interests.

As a result of the massive popularity of the United Democratic Front, the discussions concerning trade union affiliation have grown more intense. FOSATU, the Council of Unions of South Africa (CUSA), and

Dr. Halisi is a lecturer in the Political Science Department of Indiana University.

Black Labor Federations in South Africa

Congress of South African Trade Unions (COSATU)
Founded November 1985. Non-racial. Largest labor federation in South Africa. An amalgam of the National Union of Mineworkers (NUM) and FOSATU and United Democratic Front (UDF) affiliates.

Trade Union Council of South Africa (TUCSA)
Founded 1954. Multiracial. Formerly the largest federation; now being dissolved.

Federation of South African Trade Unions (FOSATU)
Founded 1979. Multiracial. Successor to Natal Trade Union Advisory Council (TUAC) of 1973. Became a part of COSATU in 1986.

Council of Unions of South Africa (CUSA)
Founded in 1980 of TUAC unions that rejected FOSATU. Affiliate of International Confederation of Free Trade Unions (ICFTU). Merged with AZACTU in 1986.

South African Congress of Trade Unions (SACTU)
Self-exiled, nonracial, acts as labor arm of the banned South African Communist Party and the African National Congress. Recognized by the International Labor Organization as the sole official representative for South African workers. Also affiliated with the World Federation of Trade Unions (WFTU).

Azanian Conference of Trade Unions (AZACTU)
Merged with CUSA in 1986.

some of the other unions maintain that there should be no formal relationship. While these unions are prepared to support specific UDF campaigns, they have resisted affiliation. Lewis argues that trade union democracy, as it was practiced during strike action, demands a committed decision by the entire trade union; therefore, the same principle should hold for worker involvement in community campaigns. FOSATU leaders point out that working class individuals are often involved in community organizations when they return home from the workplace, and indeed many black townships are company townships.

The position held by unions opposed to affiliation with community organizations should not be taken as a lack of concern with politics. First, many unions support political affiliation. Second, unions such as FOSATU are not rejecting politics but rather advocate a conception of national political organization. Some trade unionists believe that all workers should develop a national trade union center (this has come about with the formation of the Congress of South African Trade Unions), while others feel that the trade unions should be part of the national democratic movement. Both positions recognize that trade unions are not political parties but draw different conclusions from this.

Community-oriented trade union movements contend that, because they are not political parties, they must affiliate with groups such as the United Democratic Front. Unions which maintain a strict working class orientation are committed to the development of a purely working class perspective and organization. It is not that one group is apolitical and the other political: two different brands of politics are being offered.

Black Labor's Varied Political Positions

In any given country, trade union structure reflects the origins of trade union organization, ideological orientation, union policies, the nature of the employer that unions confront, and the character of government intervention. There is always a tension in trade union movements. On one hand, unions are prone to various types of sectionalism; on the other hand, broad unity is necessary in order to achieve trade union power, which in turn is needed to successfully confront employers and, at times, the state. Therefore unity becomes an important practical and ideological manifestation within trade union organizations.

Trade union movements in South Africa draw on two political traditions. One is a highly developed tradition of popular resistance and the other an equally developed tradition of trade union organization. Trade union ideology is often a mix of resistance and trade union politics. The literature suggests four broad political positions which may characterize the South African trade unions: apolitical unionism, which is most prevalent in unions formed by employers, i.e., company unions; syndicalist unionism, which distrusts all forms of bureaucracy, is rhetorically militant, and refuses any dealings with the state; black consciousness unionism, which attempts to combine black nationalist and working class objectives, but is independent of the South African Congress of Trade Unions, which is aligned with the African National Congress and also maintains a nationalist position; and working-class perspective unions, which seek to place worker power on industrial foundations to confront the state over fundamental worker rights and which do not shy away from immediate demands for reform.

The Role of White Labor Leaders

There are several kinds of white labor leaders. There are those who were previously allied with or part of the Confederation of Labor, a white conservative trade union body which never had cooperative arrangements with the black or mixed trade unions.

Even though the Confederation of Labor is at the moment politically inconsequential in that its ties to the National Party are greatly diminished, it is important.

Then there are those who have had leadership roles in white, but more often in mixed trade unions affiliated with the Trade Union Council of South Africa (TUCSA). Finally, there are the more important and more numerous whites who are part of the emerging African trade union movement. Whites play a very large role in the Federation of South African Trade Unions (FOSATU) and many of its affiliated organizations and are working cooperatively with the emergence of these new unions.

The white leadership in TUCSA is in the process of transition. In the period right after the Wiehahn Commission report when it was presumed that Africans would be organized principally in parallel unions there was confidence that the white unions would be able to incorporate Africans and that TUCSA would become the center of the trade union movement. Now white leadership sees mixed unions disaffiliating from TUCSA and aligning more and more with the new independent unions. Now white leaders are saying they have a lot to learn from the new unions. The political confidence of the TUCSA leadership has been broken by the very rapid growth of the new unions.

However, whites from TUCSA and FOSATU are definitely playing a role in the development of the African trade unions movement either through industrial councils or through organizations, such as the International Metal Federation. Increasingly these whites recognize that the real power in the trade union movement lies with the African workers.

Stanley B. Greenberg

Historically the black trade union movement has served both to radicalize and realign urban middle class politics and to absorb the economic dislocation of rural blacks mired in landlessness and migrancy. There has always been a degree of black resistance-trade union interaction, and to imagine black trade unionism without a black liberation dimension is unrealistic.

Within this context, trade unions take different ideological and political positions. This process is influenced by a union's economic structure, its industrial location, its class composition, and also the history of struggle in the various regions in which it develops. For example, trade unions in the Eastern Cape are characterized by working-class leadership and strong interaction with community organizations.

Working Class Perspective Unions

Among the "working-class perspective" unions, the Federation of South African Trade Unions (FOSATU) has the most well-developed position. Although it was initially accused of holding an apolitical stance, it would be a mistake to think of FOSATU's ideology in this light. Simply stated, FOSATU considers the popular resistance movement to be populist in character. There is often a broad working-class rhetoric, but the movement is led by middle class elites. Drawing in particular on the experiences of the Industrial and Commercial Workers' Union and SACTU, FOSATU unionists and others conclude that whenever trade unions have entered a political alliance with multi-class popular movements, workers have lost control over decisions regarding their participation. Middle class leaders have called workers to strike without considering the problems of trade union organizations. In the long run trade unions come up on the short end of such an alliance. Many unionists were inspired by the Solidarity Movement in Poland and do not want to find their unions dominated by nationalist movements or non-democratic socialist movements which undermine trade unions while upholding some abstract concept of "workers' struggle." As a result these unions are protective of the political terrain of labor and seek to make labor politics and worker interests primary.

Community-Oriented Unions

The community-oriented unions, the South African Allied Workers' Union (SAAWU) being the most exemplary, have, like the FOSATU unions, experienced a marked growth rate in the early 1980s. Unlike FOSATU unions, the community-oriented unions are general, rather than industrial. These unions more readily take up community issues and are prepared to coordinate community campaigns, such as consumer boycotts, with labor activities, such as strikes. In some instances, the consumer boycotts, organized as community campaigns, have forced recalcitrant companies into negotiations with unions. In South Africa the two major tactics of black protest are the withholding of labor and consumer power. SAAWU's reading of the situation, in contrast to FOSATU's, is that the working class has gained in political strength by forging an alliance with broad-based popular movements. However, there are tensions which develop within such alliances. For example, Thozamile Botha led the Ford Cortina workers' committee negotiations with the Ford Motor Company at the same time that he was also the head of the Port Elizabeth Black Civic Organization which was noted for its position of non-negotiation with the system. Botha had to specify that he was not talking as leader of the civic organization, but as a representative of the worker delegation. Trade union and community organization principles are not always compatible.

Community-oriented unions are concerned about being co-opted by government and employers, and they refuse to register with the government as FOSATU and the Congress of Unions of South Africa did. Although these unions recognize that they are not political instrumentalities, they feel that affiliation with community organizations helps prevent the unions from being co-opted. Community-oriented unions would agree with David Hauck, who argues that black trade unions could lead to an erosion of the apartheid labor system and assist in a transition to a non-racial capitalist equivalent, but they do not believe it is possible for the trade union movement to transform the political arena.*

Black Consciousness Unions

Recently several black consciousness unions have flourished and formed themselves into their own federation. These unions include the Black Allied Mining and Construction Workers' Union, the African Allied Workers' Union, the Insurance and Assurance Workers' Union of South Africa, and the Amalgamated Black Workers' Union. Black consciousness unions demand black leadership of the union movement and seek to combine black consciousness and trade union objectives. Interestingly, neither the black consciousness unions nor unions such as SAAWU, with its general structure, joined the new super-union federation, the Congress of South African Trade Unions. In the case of the general unions, a door was left open should they convert to an industrial structure, whereas the black consciousness unions were not invited to participate.

---

* *Black Trade Unions in South Africa* (Investor Responsibility Research Center, 1982).

Areas of Political Unity

In South Africa the trade union movement has experienced phenomenal growth since the 1970s. In addition a radicalized intelligentsia of serious proportions exists within the country. Many radical intellectuals, alienated by government policies, find a real home in the trade union movement. This politically sophisticated intelligentsia has few outlets other than community work or trade union work. There has been an explosion of intellectual involvement in the trade union movement as well as a growth of articulate political ideologies. While different positions animate trade union politics, there are broad areas of political unity. For example, all the trade unions rejected the government's attempt to impose a two-tiered labor system on black unions which would have pitted rural workers against their urban counterparts. Another example that Professor Greenberg has pointed out is the fairly unified strategy on the part of FOSATU and other unions to undermine parallel unions organized by TUCSA. The unions have a deep involvement in politics. Most of the unions, irrespective of the brand of politics they advocate, have fairly well-developed political perspectives. Few intend simply to participate in industrial reform without somehow pressing for overall democratic reform in the country.

7.

Recent Changes in the Black Labor Movement

Wilmot James

As suggested before, the South African working class is different now than it was a few decades ago. At present the majority of the African labor force is to be found in semi-skilled positions. The number in un-skilled positions, although it is difficult to define skill precisely, has been declining. In the population survey last year, semi-skilled and skilled workers were asked what their fathers' occupations were. Sixty-eight percent said that they were unskilled. There is a definite shift in terms of the occupational distribution of the working class in the African labor force.

In addition, the number of blacks that have graduated from high school has reached the level (in terms simply of numbers, not quality of education) of whites in 1980, and the number will triple by 1990. However one apportions the responsibility for these trends—whether it is government policy or the process of industrialization and capitalist development in general that is responsible—there is a definite shift in the character of the labor force.

In 1984 the number of African workers unionized was 671,000. They represent 43 percent of all unionized workers in the country.

The Development of Democratic Institutions in the Workplace

A new phenomenon in organized African labor is the develop-ment of fairly well-developed, though fragile at present, democratic in-stitutions in the workplace in the form of shop steward structures. These structures generate the working force leadership. For the first time there is an institutionalized mechanism by which labor leaders are generated on an ever-expanding scale. Up until now African leadership has come out of churches or educational institutions, but not from the framework of industrial relations and labor itself.

Dr. James is a Visiting Fellow at Yale University.

The Political Orientation of Black Labor

Robert Copp: *Do CUSA and FOSATU have any position about the economic organization of the nation? Are they committed to a free market economy?*

C. R. D. Halisi: *They have aligned themselves with the free trade unions in the West. And within the context of popular politics in South Africa, which are certainly in some ways anti-capitalist, that was a fairly principled step.*

Robert Copp: *Affiliation with the International Confederation of Free Trade Unions is not a mark of commitment to any kind of economic organization except maybe Western socialist. Is there any evidence that either CUSA or FOSATU are committed to a free market economy or do they seek a socialist economy?*

Wilmot James: *What I have seen in the unions affiliated with both CUSA and FOSATU is a commitment to workers' control. I'm not sure whether or not that means socialism. But I think that what they have in mind is greater participation of workers in decisions that previously have been considered management prerogatives.*
I have also seen a commitment, not necessarily to a free market ideology, but to free labor markets. The call for the abolition of influx control is a call for freer movement of labor. The call for abolition of pass laws is much the same thing.
There is also a commitment to making employers more

To quash romanticism about the process, I also must point out that, even though one might laud the democratic tendencies within these shop steward structures, there is also a tendency toward bureaucratization, a natural process in any kind of trade union development. In order to solidify one's position in the workplace and to become predictable and institutionalized, it is necessary to put in place efficient structures. These tend to become bureaucratized. Therefore, there is a tension between the democratic direction of the shop steward structures and the bureaucratic necessity of organization.

*accountable to worker questions, to limiting the pre-
rogatives of management and the latitude of owners in
certain areas both in the terms and conditions of work.*

*What I haven't seen is serious talk about transforming
capitalism into socialism. I haven't seen any serious con-
sideration of how one goes about the business of
transforming the capitalist economy into a socialist one.*

*I think it is fair to say that many of the trade union
and community leaders in South Africa honestly believe
that capitalism and apartheid in South Africa are inex-
tricably bound and that they have generally benefitted
one another in fundamental ways.*

Comment from the Floor: *Many people in the
trade union movement are trying to find out if capitalism
and apartheid can in any way be extricated from one
another. They are developing their own position, in terms
of worker control and worker protection and worker
rights.*

*As I understand it, some government people in the
audience are concerned that politically active South
Africans may go into the socialist camp in the effort to
reject apartheid. There is a great opportunity, if we will
seize it, to identify Western free institutions with a freer
form of political life in South Africa. If we associate
ourselves too closely with the South African government,
we won't be perceived as advocating free institutions.
There is an opportunity for the United States to define a
position separate from apartheid, but the current administration, as I understand it, is not exploring that opportunity very energetically.*

Links between Politics and the Workplace

There are essentially four forms of linkages between workplace
politics and politics outside of the workplace. The first, which is self-
evident, is the strike. It was earlier pointed out, especially by Dr.
Greenberg, that the kind of working class culture and laborist tradition
that is developing within communities becomes a support base for striking
workers. Therefore, strikes are not in any sense purely economic. They
rest on linkages between the work-place and the community.

Second, there is the stay-away. Two have taken place in the last two years, one commemorating the death of Dr. Neil Aggett. These stay-aways were not simply the product of trade union organization. In fact there was a great deal of debate and reluctance on the part of the trade unions to participate. Stay-aways can be organized very quickly and on a fairly large scale and are a testimony to the capacity of workers to halt the production machine.

Third, there has been a judicious participation and selective support for popular political questions. This support has tended to be unaffiliated, the unions shying away from direct participation in United Democratic Front or National Forum Committee politics.

The fourth form of linkage between the workplace and society outside of the workplace has been the idea of a social wage that has emerged in the last three or four years. According to its proponents,

---

Inspiration for Black Labor Unions

Question: *Where are black unions in South Africa now getting their inspiration?*

Stanley B. Greenberg: *Trade unions in South Africa are very proud that they collected funds to send to British mine workers during their strike. Workers see this as a reversal of an historic pattern of dependence on the international labor movement. There is a sense that the international labor movement looks to the black labor movement in South Africa as a vibrant movement which has something to offer to the international labor movement. Without romanticizing, one can say that this particular labor movement is operating on a peculiarly South African terrain. For example, the movement has not adopted a working class ideology at the expense of traditional African customs. The movement consciously uses songs and rural groups as part of its organization effort. The emphasis is squarely on building up democratic forums at the plant level.*

In general the inspiration comes largely from South Africa itself. There's a certain feeling of solidarity with other international organizations, but no real attempt to turn to international organizations for ideas or even for training.

workers—black workers, in particular—should attempt to bargain not for a wage based on calculations related to the workplace itself, but related to what is necessary to sustain a family as a whole. The idea of a social wage takes the bargaining process outside of the workplace and places it in a more general societal level.

Attempts at Unity and Consolidation

Since 1982 the two major federations of unions, the Federation of South African Trade Unions (FOSATU) and the Council of Unions of South Africa (CUSA), have attempted to form one federation of trade unions. Other unaffiliated unions have participated in the talks as well. Up until now they have been relatively unsuccessful, not only for policy and principle reasons but also because they represent different kinds of unionization strategies. For the most part, FOSATU represents unions organized along industrial lines, whereas CUSA is a federation of regional unions. FOSATU places a great deal of emphasis on shop stewards and entrenching the position of the union in the workplace, whereas CUSA does not. Furthermore, because of their dissimilar unionization strategies, these two federations have competed with each other over the unionization process of black labor. Therefore, unity talks have been singularly unsuccessful. My guess is that future attempts at unity between FOSATU and CUSA will be extremely difficult.

Effects of the Current Recession

It is important to point out that while the unionization process has been fairly progressive in the last four years, the recession has increased black unemployment from an already high rate prior to the recession. That means stagnant or falling wages, and that in turn means that trade union leaders will find it more and more difficult to deliver improvements to its members. Trade union leaders are finding it increasingly difficult to satisfy membership demands for high wages, better working conditions, and so on. The next three or four years will probably be fraught with extreme difficulty.

8.

Roundtable: Implications for Policy in South Africa and the United States

Stanley B. Greenberg: Contradictions in U.S. Policy

A number of speakers observed, during the course of the symposium, that there is a honeymoon period in South Africa with respect to the labor movement. However, one should be cautious about the word honeymoon because it is a "honeymoon" during which people are being detained without charge or being intimidated under various forms of legislation. Trade unions have organized widely during this period, but, at the same time, the state has continued to try to place some kind of limits on what's happening in South Africa.

U.S. policy has been shaped in this period with a fanciful notion that it is possible to reach out to the African labor movement at the same time that it is reaching out its hand in friendship to the South African state. That has been possible during this honeymoon because the labor movement has been preoccupied by enhancing its own position and creating a space for itself. As the process becomes more political, the ability of the U.S. government to maintain itself as a friend of both South African black labor and the South African state will be jeopardized. It will lead to policies that won't work and that won't serve Americans.

Robert Copp: The Sullivan Principles and Divestment

The business community does not favor the adoption of any legislation to make mandatory the voluntary Sullivan Principles under which we have been trying to operate. (It is only fair to point out, however, that Dr. Sullivan disagrees with the business position and feels that the principles can be made more broadly applicable, particularly the reporting and monitoring mechanisms, only if there is some kind of legislative sanction to back them up.) The business community feels that a massive State Department bureaucracy would be required to enforce any kind of a mandatory statutory code concerning employee relations in South Africa. Whatever may be the criticisms about its pace, reform in the relationship between management and black trade unions is on the way and is making demonstrable progress.

Another important position of the business community is that the divestment movement, as a device for putting pressure on the South African government, is ill-advised and probably would not be in the interest of the emerging black trade unions and their members in any case.

51

The Sullivan Principles

Principle I: *Nonsegregation of the races in all eating, comfort, and work facilities.*

Principle II: *Equal and fair employment practices for all employees.*

Principle III: *Equal pay for all employees doing equal or comparable work for the same period of time.*

Principle IV: *Initiation and development of training programs that will prepare, in substantial numbers, blacks and other nonwhites for supervisory, administrative, clerical, and technical jobs.*

Principle V: *Increasing the number of blacks and other nonwhites in management and supervisory positions.*

Principle VI: *Improving the quality of employees' lives outside the work environment in such areas as housing, transportation, schooling, recreation, and health facilities.*

Principle VII: *Use influence and support the unrestricted rights of black businesses to locate in the urban areas of the nation.*

Wilmot James: Four Assertions about the Future of the Black Labor Movement

My first assertion is that, despite all the very significant changes we spoke about today, and despite the fact that it appears as if the South African state and all of its institutions of control have become far less capable of ruling, and despite all the reforms that have had important consequences in certain areas of South African society, the basic parameters of that society are much the same as they were twenty or thirty years ago: homelands and the lack of black citizenship rights and political entitlements. These stand at the heart of the conflict and are still with us.

My second point is that the nature of popular opposition has clearly changed. In the past African workers and African labor played only a small role in the opposition. In the present situation labor is clearly

Principle VIII: *Influence other companies in South Africa to follow the standards of equal rights principles.*

Principle IX: *Support the freedom of mobility of black workers to seek employment opportunities wherever they exist, and make possible provisions for adequate housing for families of employees within the proximity of workers' employment.*

Principle X: *Support the ending of all apartheid laws.*

In 1977 Leon H. Sullivan, a Philadelphia clergyman and member of the board of the General Motors Corporation, persuaded twelve U.S. businesses to ascribe to six basic principles for corporations operating in South Africa. The principles have been amplified four times since then, most recently in November 1984 when the last four were added. As of October 1985 173 U.S. companies had signed (these signatories employ 60,000 persons, half of whom are black).

Each principle is accompanied by a list of specific actions that should be taken to put the principle into effect. In addition the principles call for periodic reporting on progress.

becoming the most important part of the opposition. That will change the texture of the opposition.

My third assertion is that it is clearly in the interest of African labor and black workers in general to abolish those political regulations and political institutions that have created historical disabilities. There is an interest to struggle for democratic forms of rule outside of the workplace—not in an ideological sense necessarily, but in a material sense. Once those disabilities are removed, black workers will be in a much better position to enhance their place and status both materially and socially in South African society.

Lastly, to protect the kind of space black labor has created for itself under present conditions of industrial reform, constant vigilance must be exercised to carefully guard those gains that have been made and to prevent the South African government from clamping down on African labor.

Pearl-Alice Marsh: Limitation on the Political Role of Black Labor

How do trade unions translate political issues into industrial demands? I believe that the environment in which trade unions are confined, in spite of what they would like to do as individuals or as collectives, constrains what they are able to do in the political arena. While the trade unions may provide one point of pressure on the South African government, we need not look at them as the single point, nor should community and political organizations in South Africa look to them as the major and singular point of pressure. For the decade and a half that they have been organized the trade unions have been trying to convey that message to community-based organizations.

Barbara Harmel: Change Versus True Reform

There has been a curious exchange between the Reagan Administration and the South African government as pressure has built up both in this country and in South Africa, my own country. The exchange goes like this. The U.S. government says, "Please give us change," and the South African government produces change in the Immorality Act and in the Mixed Marriages Act. Then Secretary of State George Shultz gets very excited and says, "Look, there's change!"

We must look not only at the development of the trade union movement in South Africa, but also at the degree of violence that is building up in black communities in South Africa. This administration is now being given one of its last opportunities to listen to the demands of the South African people themselves, to respond to those demands, and perhaps to save us all from a bloody conflagration, instead of accepting the South African government's "changes" that are irrelevant to the majority of people.

C. R. D. Halisi: The Dangers of Globalist Strategies in Dealing with Regional Planning

There has been a tendency on the part of some members of the Reagan Administration to favor the application of globalist perspectives to Southern Africa rather than to develop a detailed understanding of the regional dynamics. The notion that anti-communism and racial liberation are in some sort of trade-off relation is totally wrong-headed. Several scholars and African heads of state alike have contended that an unfortunate by-product of constructive engagement has been the destabilization of those countries which border South Africa. The view that South Africa is a deterrent to communist aggression is contrary to a substantial amount of evidence and analysis.

The limitations of South Africa's policy of destabilization of its neighbors and its support of dissident, anti-government movement became

Black Labor's View on the Sullivan Principles and Divestiture

Question: *What specific positions have FOSATU and CUSA and the other unions taken on making the Sullivan Principles mandatory with respect to the whole question of divestiture?*

Robert Copp: *The trade unions are basically non-supportive of the Sullivan Principles and therefore probably would not pursue mandatory Sullivan Principles as an antidote for divestment. It has been a disappointment for the Sullivan organization. Neither CUSA nor FOSATU, as the main and emerging black trade union movements, has seen any measurable benefit to them in the Sullivan Principles. They regard these principles as a gloss employed by U.S.-based companies to buttress the apartheid regime.*

Anthony G. Freeman: *I'd like to add to that. Neither CUSA nor FOSATU can formally address the question of divestment given the legal strictures in South Africa. However, their informal position has been that the divestiture campaigns are valuable pressure in the process of bringing about change in South Africa, and they have lent their moral support to those campaigns that are ongoing now in the United States.*

Robert Copp: *As I understand it, the position is something like this. "We hope that U.S. companies will not divest, but we like the movement because it puts pressure on the South African government to respond."*

rather apparent in the case of Mozambique. The South African government had to face the fact that military intervention could not in all instances substitute for a foreign policy and found itself in the ironic position of preventing the Mozambique National Resistance (MNR) from making further attacks on the Mozambique government. Like it or not, Pretoria and Washington had to face the fact that the MNR was not an anti-communist alternative to Frelimo. In the words of Simon Jenkins of the March 30, 1985, issue of the Economist, "Mr. Pik Botha doubted Renamo's ability to run anything more than a Mercedes and a few atrocities." Pretoria in this limited instance had come to grips with the axiomatic truth that regional realities were more fundamental than globalist ideology. I would hope that the administration does not attempt to employ the communist-anti-communist dichotomy to formulate policy for the removal of apartheid.

Management Personnel in American Companies
in South Africa

Question: *As late as 1972, the management of at least the American corporations represented in South Africa were obviously chosen for their ability as engineers, economists, accountants, salesmen, but rarely anybody with a record in industrial relations or personnel management. The result was that personnel policies were largely shaped by Afrikaners. Has there been a change in the type of executive chosen by American corporations? Have they overcome the strictures against the placement of non-whites in such departments as personnel or research and development?*

Robert Copp: *The director of industrial relations for Ford in South Africa is an Afrikaner, a most enlightened individual. Ford and most American companies have attempted to draw their employee relations directors from among local nationals. (Remember that one of the criticisms of American multinationals was that they always imported American labor relations objectives and tried to impose them on the host country.)*

More important than whether there has been change in the nationality of these people is that there has been a marked improvement in leadership training and development and professionalization of the personnel function in management. I think we have a much more professional and mature—not perfect by any means—management structure in employee relations than might have been true in the 1960s and early 1970s.

However, we have not done well—as a matter of fact we've done very poorly—in identifying and developing black personnel officers.

Pearl-Alice Marsh: *The general experience of management during the 1970s was that the better trained the industrial relations manager was, the better the negotiations, and the more quickly the environment got stabilized. But it is unfair to criticize just Afrikaners. Often when collective bargaining got so fierce that an official from the parent office would be called in from the United States, from West Germany, or elsewhere, often their behavior was no better than the local person who happened to be an Afrikaner.*

Stephen McDonald: *I was in South Africa during the mid-1970s in the State Department and am familiar with the type of individual referred to by the questioner. There were some dreadfully insensitive people in very critical positions in many American firms.*

Over time this has gotten considerably better, but it is very important to remember that black perspectives on the Sullivan Code effort and of American business performance are based on their experiences in the 1976-1979 period. Management personnel are more enlightened now, but it was their predecessors who set the tone and against whom black labor unions are still reacting.

Mr. McDonald was Executive Director of the United States-South Africa Leader Exchange Program at the time of the symposium.

Bibliography

Bonner, Philip. "Black Trade Unions in South Africa Since World War II" in *The Apartheid Regime,* eds. Robert Price and Carl Rosberg. Berkeley, CA: University of California, 1980.

Cheadle, Halton. "Industry and Labor: A Trade Union Perspective" in *Business in the Shadow of Apartheid,* eds. Jonathan Leape, Bo Baskin, and Stefan Underhill. Lexington, MA: Lexington Books, 1984.

Ferreira, Fred. "Industry and Labor: A Management Perspective" in *Business in the Shadow of Apartheid,* eds. Jonathan Leape, Bo Baskin, and Stefan Underhill. Lexington, MA: Lexington Books, 1984.

Freund, William. "Labor and Labor History in Africa: A Review of the Literature." *African Studies Review* 27, 2 (June 1984), pp. 1-58.

Godsell, R.M. "The Regulation of Labor" in *South Africa: Public Policy Perspectives,* ed. Robert Schrire. Cape Town: Juta and Co., 1982.

Gould, William B. "Black Unions in South Africa: Labor Law Reform and Apartheid." *Stanford Journal of International Law* 17 (Winter 1981), pp. 99-162.

Greenberg, Stanley. "Economic Growth and Political Change: The South Africa Case." *Journal of Modern African Studies* 19, 4 (1981), pp. 667-704.

Greenberg, Stanley. *Race and State in Capitalist Development: South Africa in Comparative Perspective.* New Haven, CT: Yale University Press, 1980.

Harrop, Mark D. "The Fast Ticking Bomb in South African Mines: National Union of Mineworkers: South Africa's Great Black Hope." *Business and Society Review* (Spring 1984), pp. 52-55.

Hauck, David. *Black Trade Unions in South Africa.* Washington, DC: Investor Responsibility Research Center, 1982.

International Labor Office. *Apartheid and Labor.* Geneva: 1983.

Karis, Thomas G. "Revolution in the Making: Black Politics in South Africa." *Foreign Affairs* (Winter 1983-84), pp. 378-406.

Lodge, Thomas. *Black Politics in South Africa Since 1945.* Longman, 1983.

Luckhardt, Ken, and Brenda Wall. *Organize or Starve: The History of the South African Congress of Trade Unions.* New York: International Publishers, 1980.

Marks, Shula, and Richard Rathbone, eds. *Industrialization and Social Change in South Africa.* Longman, 1983.

Marsh, Pearl-Alice. "Labor Reform and Security Repression in South Africa: Botha's Strategy for Stabilizing Racial Domination in the 1980s." *Issue* 12, 3/4 (Fall/Winter 1982), pp. 49-55.

McDonald, Steven. "A Guide to Black Politics in South Africa." *CSIS Africa Notes.* November 5, 1984.

Myers, Desaix B. *U.S. Business in South Africa: The Economic, Political and Moral Issues.* Investor Responsibility Research Center, Inc., Bloomington, IN: Indiana University Press, 1980.

Nattrass, Jill. *The South African Economy: Its Growth and Change.* Oxford, 1982.

Saunders, Christopher. "Race, Class, and South African History." *Canadian Journal of African Studies* 17, 3 (1983), pp. 555-56 (review article).

Southhall, Roger J. "Reviews." *Journal of Modern African Studies* 20, 2 (1982), pp. 323-330 (review article, including books by Greenberg and Bernard Magubane).

Biographies of the Speakers

Robert Copp is International Labor Affairs Associate in the Employee Relations Staff at the World Headquarters of Ford Motor Company in Dearborn, Michigan. He joined the Industrial Relations Staff at Ford in 1950 and has traveled widely throughout the world to assist the various Ford companies in developing and administering their labor relations programs.

He is also chairman of the U.S. Business and Industry Advisory Committee on Industrial Relations of the Organization for Economic Development and Cooperation and is a member of several committees that develop and present employer positions about industrial relations in international firms.

Mr. Copp served as the original chairman of the committee on nonsegregation and equal treatment for the International Council for Equality of Opportunity Principles, which oversees application of the Sullivan Principles in South Africa. That committee developed the Sullivan organization's approach to black labor unions.

Anthony G. Freeman was designated Special Assistant to the Secretary and Coordinator of International Labor Affairs of the Department of State in August 1983. Prior to joining the Foreign Service in July of 1961, he was a labor economist at the U.S. Department of Labor.

His State Department labor assignments have included Labor Counselor in Rome (1980-1983), Labor Attache in Buenos Aires (1976-1980), Labor Attache in La Paz (1967-1970) and Deputy to the Bureau of American Republics Affairs Regional Labor Advisor and Assistant Labor Attache in Buenos Aires (1962).

Robert S. Gelbard is currently Director of the Office of Southern African Affairs at the State Department, a post he has held since June 1984. A career Foreign Service officer, he joined the Department of State in 1967. From 1982 to 1984, he was Deputy Director and Acting Director of the Office of Western European Affairs. From 1978 to 1982, he was First Secretary, in charge of Economic and Financial Affairs, in Paris. From 1976 to 1978, he was a financial economist in the Office of Regional Political and Economic Affairs within the Bureau of European Affairs.

Mr. Gelbard served as a member of the U.S. delegation to the Conference on International Economic Cooperation in Paris from 1976 to 1977 and in a part-time capacity on the Council of Economic Advisors from 1977 to 1978.

Stanley B. Greenberg is Associate Director of the Southern African Research Program at Yale University, a position he has held since 1975. He is also Visiting Scholar at the Harry S. Truman Research Institute for the Advancement of Peace at Hebrew University and Research Affiliate at the Center for International and Area Studies at Yale.

From 1982 to 1984, he was Visiting Associate Professor in the Department of Political Science at Ohio Wesleyan University. Prior to that post, he was a lecturer in the Department of African-American Studies and the Council on International and Area Studies at Yale.

He has published widely on Africa. Among his most recent works are: *Legitimizing the Illegitimate: State, Markets and the South African Working Class* (forthcoming) and "Managing Class Structures in South Africa" in Irving Markovitz's *Studies in Power and Class in Africa.*

C. R. D. Halisi is currently a lecturer in the Political Science Department of Indiana University, a post he has held since 1983. He is also lecturer and Assistant Coordinator of the African Politics Seminar at the Immaculate Heart College in Los Angeles.

In 1982 he was a Teaching Fellow in the Political Science Department at the University of California in Los Angeles and lecturer in the Political Science Department at California State College.

Dr. Halisi has spoken and published widely on African affairs. Among his most recent works are "Political Science and Africa" with James S. Coleman, a paper presented at the African Studies Association Conference in Washington, D.C., in 1982, published in the *African Studies Review* (September-December 1983) and "Black Consciousness and Political Realignment," a paper presented at the Social Science Research Council Joint Committee on African Studies Conference in New York in 1982. Dr. Halisi's Ph.D. dissertation was entitled *The Dynamics of Black Politics in South Africa.*

Barbara Harmel is Director of the U.S. Africa Commission at the Center for Development Policy in Washington, D.C. She has been associated with the Southern Africa Research Program at Yale University since 1978.

She was born and raised in South Africa and has been in political exile since 1964. She has completed her Ph.D. at Essex University where her award is pending. She prepared her dissertation on "Political Restructuring and Black Response in South Africa, 1948-1960."

Wilmot James has been a Visiting Fellow at Yale University since 1984. He has taught most recently at the University of the Western Cape in South Africa.

Dr. James has done research and published on a variety of issues on political sociology in the Republic of South Africa. He is currently working on a comparative analysis of gold production and labor markets.

Pearl-Alice Marsh is currently a Ford Foundation Fellow in International Affairs at the Institute for International Studies at the University of California at Berkeley, a position she has held since 1984. Prior to this post, she was a Fellow at the Hoover Institution at Stanford University in California, from 1983 to 1984.

She has written "Labor Reform and Security Repression in South Africa," published in *Issue* (the African Studies Association Journal) and "A South African Journey," published in *Journal of Women and Religion* (Winter 1982).

Steven McDonald was Executive Director of the United States-South Africa Leader Exchange Program (USSALEP) from 1982 to 1986. USSALEP was founded by a group of Americans and South Africans in 1958 to encourage the development of a just society. It has its headquarters in Washington, D.C.

From 1979 to 1982, Mr. McDonald taught International Affairs at Drury College in Missouri. From 1970 to 1979, he was a Foreign Service officer in the State Department. He served exclusively in the Africa Bureau and was posted in Uganda from 1971 to 1973, and Pretoria, South Africa, from 1976 to 1979. He also served as Country Desk officer for Angola, Mozambique, and Guinea-Bissau from 1973 to 1975.

Ronald Palmer is currently assigned as a Visiting Scholar and Senior Foreign Affairs Fellow at the Center for Strategic and International Studies at Georgetown University. He served as Ambassador to Malaysia from 1981 to 1983 and to Togo from 1976 to 1978.

After entering the Foreign Service in 1957, Ambassador Palmer served in Djakarta, Kuala Lumpur, Copenhagen, Manila, and Lome.

Diane B. Bendahmane, the editor of this volume, is a Washington-based editor and publications specialist with experience in international relations and development assistance. She has worked for the Carnegie Endowment for International Peace, *Foreign Policy* quarterly, Appropriate Technology International, the Peace Corps, the World Health Organization and a number of consulting firms and nongovernmental organizations.